OUR FATHER

A ONE-MONTH DEVOTIONAL GUIDE TO DISCOVERING THE

FIRST PERSON OF THE TRINITY

OUR FATHER

Este libro es dedicado a mis hermanos y hermanas en Quiebra Hacha.

"Our Father in heaven,
hallowed be your name.
Your kingdom come,
your will be done,
on earth as it is in heaven.
Give us this day our daily bread,
and forgive us our debts,
as we also have forgiven our debtors.
And lead us not into temptation,
but deliver us from evil."

Matthew 6:9-13

ISBN-13: 978-0-9849983-0-2 (MJC Media)

ISBN-10: 0984998306

Preface

Who is God, really? In a previous Devotions for Disciples book we asked the question "Who is Jesus?" because so often people don't have a clear understanding of the Son of God. But do we really understand the Father any more than we do the Son? What is He like? Is He an angry God of wrath that seeks to punish us for our sins? Is He a loving Father who cares about our every need? Can He possibly be both?

In this devotional guide we're going to look at what God says about Himself in the Bible. What He chooses to reveal (and not reveal) about himself is very important for us to look at. Sometimes we base our ideas about Him on what other people have told us or even what we've seen in cartoons. Come on, admit it, at least once you've thought of God as what you learned about Him from Looney Tunes.

The truth is, God wants us to know Him. The Father is such a major part of the biblical writings that we can learn so much about His character and what He wants from us by reading and studying. The more we know about who He is, the more we can know what our purpose in this life is. The more we know Him, the more we love Him. But we need to seek that knowledge. He's not hiding. He's made Himself known right there in the pages of our text.

Let's take a look and see what it says.

May God bless you as you seek more of Him.

Matthew J. Cochran

He is the beginning of all things

Isaiah 44:6 Thus says the Lord, the King of Israel and his Redeemer, the Lord of hosts: "I am the first and I am the last; besides me there is no god."

Let's start at the very beginning. We want to know all the answers of life but we often start in the wrong place in asking. Creation didn't begin with me or you, but sometimes we treat the world as though that's the case. We don't intentionally put ourselves at the center of the universe, but there we are, thinking that we are the first to exist.

But before there was anything, anything at all, there was God. He existed in three distinct persons made up of the same essence. Trying to explain the Trinity is nearly impossible, but suffice it to say that the Father was there before time and He created all things. He was in control then and He still is today.

All things find their beginning in Him, not just the earth and all that came into being "in the beginning". All things. You're here because God made you. Science and discoveries are in existence because God made it so. Nothing, not one little molecule, is created without His hand at work.

Look back at the creation account in Genesis and think about it in light of the fact that even things this very day are here because of God. How does it make you see the world differently? How does it make you view your life specifically and your purpose?

Father, I thank you that you are my Lord and my God. I know that all things came about because you made it so and I know that you hold all things together. Help me to trust that you are the God who was, and is, and is to come.

Amen

He is eternal

Psalm 102:27 but you are the same, and your years have no end.

Sometimes I get scared. I worry that life won't work out for some reason or another. It may be that an unforeseen circumstance has changed my plans or that I just don't know how something could possibly turn out ok. Then I remind myself that God is still in control. There's something about knowing this that brings peace.

The thing is, there's never any time that we have a real reason to worry about anything. God is in control, yes, but what's more is that He's in control of things forever. He won't disappear one day and leave us stranded. We don't need to keep all of our ducks perfectly in a row in order for Him to remain God. He was, He is, and He is to come.

All things find there beginnings in Him, but we can also rest assured that He'll bring them through to their completion. We're safe because He's eternal. We can put our worries on Him because He can handle them. Nothing is too big for Him, nothing is too hard. He's the one who made everything and He's the one who contains everything.

So I get scared sometimes just like I'll bet you do and the only way to know that there's nothing to fear is to remember that God is God and He always will be. He'll never fail and He'll never leave. He's eternal, and that makes all the difference in the world.

Father, thank you for reminding me in your Word that you are eternal. I never have to worry that you'll go away because you are greater than time itself. Help me to be mindful of the fact that you are with me always and forever.

Amen

He Created

Genesis 1:1 In the beginning, God created the heavens and the earth.

Any discussion of God the Father has to begin...in the beginning. And so there we've begun. God existed before there was time and then, He created time. This is confusing to almost anyone, but the basis of discussing God is the creation of time and all things in existence. Before He spoke it, it didn't exist.

Clearly, Jesus played a role in creation. Colossians and the Gospel of John make that very clear. But God the Father has the authority to speak things into existence, and so it was with the creation of the world. He spoke, and there was light. He spoke and there was night and there was day. He spoke, and His words were so powerful that whatever He said happened. Now why is it again that we question whether God is powerful enough to help us in our lives?

There was nothing but Him, and then there was what He created. That's pretty simple, yet it's so incredibly complicated. How did God exist from eternity if nothing else existed? How did creation take place? Was it a big bang? These are honestly mysteries that aren't going to be answered easily. We can never know everything about God, but we do know this, our Father set the universe in place, and all things hold together because of Him. He's always going to be there to keep things going. We can rely on Him for all of our lives' issues because He can handle all things at once.

Father, thank you for your goodness. Thank you for choosing to create and to include me among your creation. I know that all you do is good and all of your creation is planned out and exists for a purpose. Help me to trust this and put my faith in you for all things.

Amen

He is sovereign

Psalm 103:19 The Lord has established his throne in the heavens, and his kingdom rules over all.

No one is above God. Not the most powerful king or the strongest nation. No amount of military might or earthly knowledge can overcome Him. He alone is in control. We'll unpack this idea of sovereignty more as we go along and how it plays out in our lives.

Here's how this pertains specifically to the Father: God the Father establishes His will, the purposes He wants to accomplish. The Son, Jesus, though He's equally God, submits to the will of the Father and carries out the plan. The Holy Spirit, also equally God, works in and through people to make things happen. That's a lot to think about, but here's the deal: God is in ultimate control.

As followers of Christ we're called to submit our lives to Him in order to bring about the Father's purposes. We each have a role to play in this life on earth and we've been given specific talents and abilities, we've even been put in specific places, to do what God wants us to do. The plan is all put together by God the Father. It's our job to follow Jesus in doing what the Father has for us to do with those talents, time, and circumstances.

Nothing in this life is pure coincidence. God has His eyes on what's going on and He can work through whatever He wants to use for His own purpose and His own glory. Trust Him. He's got it under control.

Sovereign Lord, forgive me for the times that I haven't trusted you and had the faith that you have all things under control. Please help me to follow after your plan even when it seems to make little sense to me.

Amen

He is all-knowing

Psalm 147:4-5 He determines the number of the stars; he gives to all of them their names. Great is our Lord, and abundant in power; his understanding is beyond measure.

The same God who created all things knows you personally. The very same God that Jesus called Father is your Father as well. He knows every star in the sky, every bird in the air, and yet He takes the time to know you and everything about you.

Do you ever wonder if God is listening to you? Does it ever seem like He just doesn't care or that He isn't hearing you? What you need to know is that the Father does hear you and He does care. He cares so much that sometimes He doesn't answer your prayer the way you'd like. He's able to see all things, past, present, and future, and that means He knows what the best action is in response to your requests. He cares so much that He sometimes says no.

Don't ever think that God doesn't know what's going on with you. He doesn't sleep at the wheel. He's always present with you, no matter what you're going through, and He knows your needs, your circumstances, and your pain. He wants to get you through it, but you need to trust that He knows best how to do that.

He sees you. He hears you. He loves you. And He works all things out for good because He knows how it all turns out in the end.

Our Father, thank you for caring for me, even though you own the cattle on a thousand hills, even though you know every star by name. Thank you for hearing my prayers and listening to my heart.

Amen

He Calls

1 Corinthians 1:9 God is faithful, by whom you were called into the fellowship of his Son, Jesus Christ our Lord.

We like to make much of what we do for God and what we've done to change since becoming Christians, but we leave out how much of the work was done by God himself. Much of what we take credit for was initiated by Him and we merely carried out what He called us to do. Let's step aside for the moment and consider His calling.

God calls us into fellowship with himself through Jesus. He wants us to be His. He's a loving Father who adores us and would have us all follow Him in love. He calls us into good works. He wants to see us do something with our faith, not just believe but show our love for Him by serving others and serving Him. We're His vessels here on earth to do His will, but it requires us letting Him have control of the wheel.

He calls us to repentance. God wants us to seek after Him with a sorrow for the things we've done to keep us from Him. We can't serve sin and God, so when it comes down to it, He's calling us to genuinely give up the sin and follow Him. He calls us to holiness. We can't be perfect, but we can be in a right relationship with God through Christ. Holiness and righteousness are His in which to cloak us and we receive them when we follow Him. He calls each of us to ministry. Not all of us will leave our careers and become pastors and preachers, but we all have a ministry in which God can use us to expand His kingdom and bring glory unto himself.

He's calling even now. There's something tugging on your heart that you know you ought to do. You read something in God's Word that the Holy Spirit emphasized in your heart. You are being called and your response does not mean that you are doing anything on your own. Your answer to the call is out of obedience.

Lord, I know that you have called me because I'm yours. Thank you for working in me and through me by way of your Holy Spirit. Thank you for guidance and direction. Help me to always follow in obedience.

Amen

He is all-powerful

Jeremiah 32:27 "Behold, I am the Lord, the God of all flesh. Is anything too hard for me?

Omnipotence. There's a word that just can't be used when talking about anything but God. There's no one and no thing in this whole world that has absolute power over all things, except God. Only He has the power to create the world and to then hold it in place. Only He can tell the sun when to come out and the oceans where they stop.

It's important for us to know that God is all-knowing because we need to understand that He's a God who hears us and knows us. But we also need to fully grasp the belief that He's capable of all things. It's one thing to believe that He's got the knowledge of what to do, it's another to believe that He's capable of doing it. It's the difference between real faith and religious faith.

What are you praying for right now? What have you asked for that you need to believe God can deliver? Are you praying with the knowledge that He can do it or are you praying in hopes that He can do it? Know this: God can do all things. Never pray with fear that He won't be powerful enough to make good on His promises. He's powerful enough to create all things out of nothing, powerful enough to hold all of creation in place, and powerful enough to answer every prayer we could ever offer up to Him.

We have not because we ask not. It isn't because our Father can't provide. Nothing is too hard for Him.

Father, nothing is too hard for you. You can truly do all things. Nothing stands against you and nothing is impossible for you. Please help me to remember this as I pray. Help me to pray with the faith that you can provide anything and everything.

Amen

He is unfathomable

Isaiah 55:8 For my thoughts are not your thoughts, neither are your ways my ways, declares the Lord.

We live in an age where there is so much information right at our fingertips. We have so much available to us that it can seem like an infinite amount. If we're not careful we can think we've got everything figured out. We can start to think that we don't even need God because we know everything to know.

But the truth is we have only a tiny fraction of the knowledge that's possible. Even though it seems like there's nothing left to discover, God has secrets we could never even dream of. He's so incredibly big compared to us and He has so much more than He's revealed.

Our human minds wouldn't even be able to handle all that God knows. We'd explode if we actually caught a glipse of the mysteries He's withheld from us. We honestly won't ever even know everything there is to know about all of the things that ARE available to us in this life.

The next time you think you know better than God and get angry that He doesn't act according to your vast wisdom, pause. Think for a minute about how massive God is, about how much more there is than what we have learned here.

Put your trust in the Father that He knows more than you will ever know and He chooses to act according to what He knows, not what you know. Be thankful that He doesn't do things according to your ways, but according to His ways!

Lord, though I will never fully understand your ways, I will trust in you. I will trust in your nature and in your goodness. Your ways and not my ways and I will have faith that you know what's best for me.

Amen

He Commissions

Matthew 9:38 therefore pray earnestly to the Lord of the harvest to send out laborers into his harvest.

We're not only called by God, but we're sent by Him as well. He calls us to be what He wants us to be and He sends us to do what He would have done. God can do anything He wants in this world because He is all-powerful, but He chooses to use people to carry out His purposes in most cases. We have the privilege of bearing the commission of the Lord.

When considering what it means to be commissioned, it's important that we realize it's more than just being sent. The word commission carries with it the authorization of the sender, and even the granting of power to perform the duties one is commissioned to do. Our Lord does not just send us, He empowers us to accomplish every act and every goal. One who is commissioned acts on behalf of the one who sent them.

Jesus is the perfect example of carrying out the will of the Father in humble submission. He was sent to do a task and He completed it, just as the Father commissioned Him to do. He was sent, equipped, and protected as He lived out the Father's mission for Him.

The one who sends us is the Most High God, the creator and sustainer of all things. He holds the universe in balance and He is more than capable of giving us what we need to succeed. If we make ourselves available to do what He calls us to do, He will send us and equip us for the task. He will look after us.

Father, help me to carry out the purpose you've called me to by walking on the path you've laid out before me. Help me to keep to your ways and live out my commission. I submit myself to you.

Amen

He is our refuge

Psalm 18:2 The Lord is my rock and my fortress and my deliverer, my God, my rock, in whom I take refuge, my shield and the horn of my salvation, my stronghold.

Where do you turn when things get tough?   Your answer to that question reveals a lot about your faith.   Do you put your trust in things that can't deliver?   Do you find comfort from that which cannot guarantee it? There's only one safe place to turn. God is our refuge.

The very same God who spared Noah's family from the flood, delivered His people into the promised land, defeated an army using only 300 men, and sent a Savior to earth will be there in your struggles.   He's there for you in your loss, in your surprising diagnosis, your layoff, or your broken relationship.   You can turn to Him when you're hurt, afraid, worried, depressed, confused, or unsure. He's been there.   He understands your needs, frustrations, and heart-felt desires.

Your heavenly Father can deliver on anything because He owns it all. Most of all, He can provide comfort.   That other stuff - money, therapy, alcohol - none of them make a good refuges in which to take shelter.   Only in the arms of your loving Father can you truly be safe and secure.   He loves you, He cares for you, and He's available anytime you need Him.

Father, I turn to you. Only you can provide me with the safety and shelter that I need. Only you can keep me from my enemies and protect me from all harm. I trust in you.

Amen

He is our comfort

Psalm 23:4 Even though I walk through the valley of the shadow of death, I will fear no evil, for you are with me; your rod and your staff, they comfort me.

If we take refuge in the Lord, we'll find comfort.   But what is comfort, really?   It seems that maybe we've been taught the wrong idea about what this means.   Advertising has taught us that we deserve comfort, but none of the earthly things that we describe as comfortable even come close to the comfort our Father provides.

One dictionary says that to comfort is to "give strength or hope to." That's a great way to look at God's comfort.   He gives us strength when we're weak.   He gives us hope when we have none.   If you think about it, there really is nothing else in this whole world that can truly offer hope.   Everything we turn to for hope - religion, science, politics - it all just falls apart in the end.   There's no real hope to be had in them.

The Creator and Sustainer of all things, the Alpha and Omega - He brings real hope because He's the only one capable of actually being there for us no matter what.   If you want real comfort from all that this life throws at you, stop turning to all those places that lack and turn to the real Comforter. In Him there's hope.

Father, I know that only you can truly provide comfort. None of the other places I look to comfort me can provide what I need. Thank you for caring for me and giving me rest when I need it. You are the great Comforter and in you alone do I put my trust.

Amen

He Protects

Psalm 23:4 Even though I walk through the valley of the shadow of death, I will fear no evil, for you are with me; your rod and your staff, they comfort me.

Our loving heavenly Father watches over His flock and will not lose even one without knowing about it. There's nowhere that we can go where we'll be outside His sight and His protection. He can and does protect us. We have nothing to fear.

The things of this world can be dangerous to anyone, but to a follower of Christ, some of them are downright disastrous outside the grace of God. He keeps us from harm and allows nothing to prosper against us as we carry out His purposes. If we're on the path He sets us on, we'll see plenty of opposition, but He'll be the One who keeps us going, guarding us all the way.

He know our weaknesses and won't allow us to face more temptation than we can bear. In fact, when faced with temptation, God provides us a way out! He gives us the avenue to get away from it, because He cares about our future. He has things for us to do and He'll provide a way for us to make it to the finish line. He's there for us, even when it sometimes seems He's not. He's never off duty, He's always watching over us, like a shepherd who cares about each and every one of his little sheep.

Father, thank you for watching over me and keeping me safe from harm. I know that you have me in your sight so I have nothing to fear. Help me when I'm afraid to remember that you're always with me.

Amen

He is our portion

Psalm 73:26 My flesh and my heart may fail, but God is the strength of my heart and my portion forever.

Sometimes the authors that penned the words of the Bible, given to them by the Holy Spirit, wrote in such a way that even modern day translators struggle to relate into terms we use now. For instance: What does it mean that God is our *portion*? This word is used many times throughout Scripture, but sometimes we pass over it without grasping its real depth.   God is our portion - and that means everything.

What do we "get" in exchange for giving our lives over to God? Some would answer that we get forgiveness or eternal life, others would say peace or even "whatever we ask for." The answer to what we get when we give our lives to God is we get God. Really, He's our prize. He's our treasure. Nothing else compares. Having God is having it all. He's the Creator and Sustainer of all things - and He's ours.

The things of this world that we work so hard to obtain and then to hold onto fail to satisfy us. They just leave us wanting to obtain and hold onto more things. Only the life-giver can really give us what we really need. He gives us Himself.

Father, thank you for giving the greatest gift of all. By giving Yourself I know that I have all I need and will never be in want of anything. I don't need more stuff, I just need you.

Amen

He is ever-present

Psalm 46:1 God is our refuge and strength, a very present help in trouble.

Wherever you go, there you are. No matter where you are, you're not alone. God is with you. He's with you in your times of triumph and in your times of trouble. He's there when you're doing well and He's there when you've never needed Him more.

Sometimes we think that God isn't around when things get really bad-like He's only available to help us with issues that don't require a lot from Him. We think He cares enough to help in the little troubles but those big ones are just too much. When that's our attitude, we don't even ask Him. We don't bother to pray.

Other times it may be that we think our trouble is too small. God has bigger things to worry about. Why would He care about my mundane issue? I'm sure I'd just be taking God away from doing something more important if I prayed about this.

But the truth is God is always present. No matter how big or how small our problems - or our victories - may be, He is there. He cares about the minute details and the earth-shattering events alike. No matter where we go, we haven't lost Him or bored Him. He's our ever-present help in times of trouble.

I'm so thankful, Father, that you never leave my side. You're always with me, no matter what I'm going through. Nothing happens without your knowledge and you want what's best for me. Thank you for being with me, no matter what.

Amen

He Provides

Matthew 6:11 Give us this day our daily bread.

We all have needs. Every one of us has something that we can't live without, even if it's only the basics of food and water. But no matter what our needs may be, they are supplied by our Father in heaven. All good gifts are from above. (James 1:17)

What's more, God knows what we need before we do. He's aware of our everyday necessities and even our desires. He provides not only what we need to survive, but to thrive and to carry out His purposes. If He calls us to it, He'll equip us to carry it out. We're never left without the required tools and skills to be used by God. He's always ready to give.

Though He knows what we need, in some cases God does want us to ask of Him what we seek. It may be at times that He gives out of His grace and we never even knew to ask. It may, however, be at times that He withholds something from us until we petition Him. This is His prerogative, but it's done to keep us aligned with His will. If we ask what He wills, it will certainly be given.

Even when we don't know what to ask, God provides for us through the Holy Spirit's petitioning on our behalf. He truly is a Father who is watching out for His children, ready to give them all that they need.

Thank you, Father, for caring for me as your child. Thank you for providing me what I need and keeping from me what is not in my best interest. I know that I'll never need anything with you as my Father.

Amen

He is our Father

1 John 3:1a See what kind of love the Father has given to us, that we should be called children of God; and so we are.

The Bible is the resource God chose in which to reveal Himself to us. In it He tells us about His character, His will, His work, and His gospel message of redemption and salvation. It's interesting that all throughout, God chose to use familial language to make Himself known. Bear in mind that no word within Scripture goes without purpose.

Jesus is the Son, we are adopted children of the Father. Why does He speak this way? Why our Father? Some of us have great earthly fathers who we look up to, others have fathers who are so terrible that they aren't worth thinking about. Still others had fathers who were downright absent. Forget what you think about your dad. God is unlike any dad we know, good or bad, here on earth. He loves at all times, even when we don't obey. He never fails, He always listens, He doesn't make promises He won't keep.

God is loving and just, never giving punishment apart from our benefit from it. He's in control of all things and yet He takes the time to look after all of the needs of His children. He's truly a Father to us- far greater than we can ever expect the very best earthly father to be.

My Father, thank you for loving me as only you can. Thank you for adopting me into your family, caring for me, keeping me, providing for me, and looking after me. I desire to be the child you want me to be.

Amen

He is worthy to be praised

Psalm 145:3 Great is the Lord, and greatly to be praised, and his greatness is unsearchable.

Nobody's perfect, right? Nobody is truly worthy of being praised. Well, not exactly. There is only one who is worthy of all honor we could possibly ever give Him and then infinitely more. The God of the universe, our Father, is worthy to be praised.

It's not all about what He does for us - for that we give Him thanks. No, what we praise Him for is simply who He is. Just His character alone makes Him worthy of worship. So who *is* He?

He's the beginning of all things, the eternal Creator, the sovereign and omniscient Lord who calls, commissions, protects, and provides. He's omnipotent and omnipresent, the first among equals in the Trinity, knowable and yet unknowable, a place to find refuge and comfort.

He's our portion, our treasure, our Father who adopts us into His family, so good and great and just that He disciplines us for our own sake. He makes no mistakes, shapes all things and brings all things to completion. He's a holy judge who is patient and rules out of love. He is awesome. And He is worthy of all praise and honor and glory - forever and ever.

Father, you and you alone are worthy of all praise and honor and glory. You created all things, are above all things, and keep all things in balance. To you be all praise.

Amen

He Adopts

Galatians 4:6 But when the fullness of time had come, God sent forth his Son, born of woman, born under the law, to redeem those who were under the law, so that we might receive adoption as sons.

Christian, you have been chosen. Just as an adopted child is chosen by his parents, so too have you been chosen by God and given all the rights due one of His children. Women shouldn't be put off by the masculine language here. It's good that we're all called "sons" of God, despite our gender, because the firstborn son in any first century family who would have been reading this letter written by Paul would have had an abundance of rights that the other children would not have had. We should all be pleased to be called sons of God.

He has adopted us into His family through His Son, Jesus Christ. Through Jesus' life, death on the cross, and resurrection from the dead, God sent an invitation to us to be part of the family. When we respond, the adoption is final and we gain child status. The adopted children of God have rights to everything the firstborn has as co-heirs with Christ.(Romans 8:17)

Not everyone is a child of God, though He created everyone. Only those who belong to Him through faith in Jesus Christ are His adopted children. But if you are His, take comfort in the knowledge that He chose you to be part of His family. Even while you were still just a sinner, He chose you and called you to Himself. He loves you that much.

Father, thank you for choosing to adopt me, even though I was just a sinner who had no worth. Thank you for showing me love as only you can. Truly, you are my Father.

Amen

He is good

Psalm 107:1 Oh give thanks to the Lord, for he is good, for his steadfast love endures forever!

When praying and asking God for direction or provision or any other thing, we have to have one thing in mind. He is good. When we pray but fear that God doesn't care or isn't a loving Father, we tend to pray without expectation.

But when we pray knowing that God is a good and loving Creator who cares about the lives of His children, our heart's attitude is one of belief and faith. Knowledge that God is good changes things. Looking to Him knowing of His goodness gives us peace and comfort.

Some think that God is on high watching and waiting to strike us down with punishments. But that's not Him. He's not evil and has no evil intentions. He's good and when we do face discipline it's because He cares enough for us to correct us - so that we'll be better for it. When He makes us wait for something, it's not because He is being cruel. It's because He's good.

All good things come from God[*]. In Him there is no evil[†]. Not a thing that our Father does is for the wrong reasons. Do you trust in that? Put your faith in a good and loving God who cares so much for you that He would send His Son to die in your place. He is good - all the time.

---

[*] James 1:17

[†] Psalm 92:15

Father, thank you for revealing yourself in Scripture so that I can know your character. Because I know that you're good, I can trust you with all things. Because you have my best future in mind, I know that there's no reason to worry.

Amen

He is great

Psalm 145:3 Great is the Lord, and greatly to be praised, and his greatness is unsearchable.

How great is our God? To what heights and what depths and what lengths do His greatness measure? Truth be told, we'll never know. Our minds can't handle just how great God is - this is why we owe Him all of our praise.

He's everywhere at all times, He's existed since before there was time, He can do all things. Who are we to think we're anything in the shadow of who God is? The comparison of ants on the ground to us in the sky looking down does not justice to our relationship to God. We are nothing and He is everything.

And yet, in His goodness He's chosen to make us something. Through Christ we're made into children of God, coheirs of the spiritual blessings owed only to Jesus. He knows all that will happen and chooses to intervene in our lives. He can do anything He wants, yet He comes down to deal with His people.

He knows every star by name, holds the world in His hands, sees the heart of every man, woman and child. He is great above all things. And He's our Father.

Father, you are mighty! You are above all things and nothing can defeat you! Truly, you are great! All of my praise goes out to you that you may be glorified.

Amen

He Disciplines

Hebrews 12:7-8 It is for discipline that you have to endure. God is treating you as sons. For what son is there whom his father does not discipline? If you are left without discipline, in which all have participated, then you are illegitimate children and not sons.

How does a child learn to do what's right? They learn through the example their parents give, yes, but they also learn through correction and discipline when they do the wrong things. By being taught what the rights things are and disciplined over the wrong things, a child can grow into maturity, knowing right from wrong.

How does a Christian learn what God wants? We have Jesus as our example and we have the commandments to guide us in what's right. But when we stray from what God has taught us doesn't He also correct us? Doesn't He sometimes put us back on the right track because He loves us? There's a big difference between punishment and discipline. Some have the view that God is up above watching for us to mess up so He can take His vengeance on us. That action out of anger would be punishment. But God doesn't punish those He loves. He disciplines them.

The truth is, we may not always even know we're being disciplined. The Father may remove something from us that isn't good for us in a way that provides correction. We may not even have been aware of what happened. God may also put people in our lives at certain times that give some correction. Whatever the method, God disciplines because He loves. Any parent who provides no guidance and no boundaries to their children does not love them. If a child is allowed to destroy themselves, the parent has no love for them. But our Father does love us, and He loves us enough to make sure we're everything we're supposed to be.

My Father, thank you for your correction. I know that if you didn't discipline me it would mean you didn't love me. You know what's best for me, even when I think I'm the one who knows what I need. Thank you for loving me enough to show me the right way.

Amen

He is perfect

Matthew 5:48 You therefore must be perfect, as your heavenly Father is perfect.

You've heard that there's nothing that God can't do, but this isn't completely true. God cannot make a mistake. He is perfect.

There's just something that's liberating about recognizing the fact that our heavenly Father doesn't make mistakes. When I'm parenting my own kids, I sometimes make wrong choices. Sometimes I discipline too harshly. Other times I'm too lenient and let my kids do things that I later realize were not a good idea. I learn from those mistakes, but I'm in awe of the fact that God doesn't need to learn from such things. He never gets it wrong.

No doubt there are times that we don't agree with the way God's done something, but that doesn't mean He's wrong. It means we don't fully understand His ways. But when we really embrace the notion that God is without error, it brings freedom. Knowing that a sovereign God who knows all things that are going on in your life is also incapable of messing anything up is life-changing. There's peace in that.

We can pray knowing that when we get an answer it's from an all-knowing Father and that He is correct in whatever way He chose to answer. There's no sense in arguing with Him over the outcome because He's never, ever wrong. He's perfect in all His ways.

When He created you, He did it without making a single mistake. You were made with a purpose by a God who is perfect.

Father, I know that nothing that comes from you can be false. Nothing from you can be a lie or a mistake. You know all things and are incapable of being wrong. I put my trust in you, knowing that your way is the right way.

Amen

He is the end of all things

Revelation 21:6 And he said to me, "It is done! I am the Alpha and the Omega, the beginning and the end. To the thirsty I will give from the spring of the water of life without payment.

Do you ever fear the future? Are you afraid to give any thought to what will happen to this world when the end comes? Are you thinking right now as you read this that the end times already have come?

The Bible has a lot to say about how things end, some of them may seem a little unnerving because of their unfamiliar nature (flying creatures with eyes on their wings and whatnot), but there's great news about it all. God is the author of all things, from creation to His appointed end time.

There's nothing to worry about! Nothing ends apart from the way God wants it to come to completion. None of it ought to scare us. Even though there's talk of earthquakes and the sky becoming dark, wars, and famines, we know who is in control of it all. We know who wrote the ending before the beginning.

God is good, He is in control, He is perfect in all His ways. He will bring all things to their necessary completion for your life, for my life, and for the world as we know it. Keeping in mind the nature and character of the Father alleviates fear of the future.

Father, I won't fear the future because I know that you hold the future in your hands. You created all and none of it will come to an end without your say. Even my own life is within your grasp.

Amen

He Shapes

Isaiah 64:8 But now, O Lord, you are our Father; we are the clay, and you are our potter; we are all the work of your hand.

What does God want from us?   Sometimes we need but ask Him. We'll find many times that He's already at work in us to bring about His purposes.   We are His instruments in this life, if we've given ourselves over to Him...and really even if we haven't (Romans 9:20-23).   He makes us into what He needs us to be, what He wants us to be.

We all have our own desires and our own ideas about what being godly means, but it's God himself who determines what our strengths and weaknesses are, what our opportunities will be, what our roles in life will be.   But we get to where we are in His great plan one step at a time, one little minor change at a time.   We experience and encounter things that develop us as a people and then we in turn become a little bit more of what God intended.   If we're following Christ, we'll be used for good.   God will have us play out a role on His team.   The wicked and ungodly play a role too in His plan, but not for the same side.

Pray for wisdom, pray that God the Father would work on you to make you into the creation He intended you to be.   Seek to be more like Christ, in His character and in His devotion to the Father.   Let God work in you and through you as He shapes you into a fine piece of art.

You've known me from before the time I was born and you've shaped me to be the person I am today. You have caused me to be exactly who you want me to be. Thank you for your great work in me, Father.

Amen

He is holy

Isaiah 5:16 But the Lord of hosts is exalted in justice, and the Holy God shows himself holy in righteousness

Isn't God being holy pretty much the same thing as Him being perfect? Well, yeah, it is. But this attribute of God could never fully be covered, no matter what amount of time we spend on it. God's holiness and perfection are just so beyond our understanding that our words are not enough to describe it.

To be holy is to be "set apart." When we talk about God being perfect, think about the fact that no one else is perfect. You and I are messed-up, fallen people who make mistakes, do selfish things, hurt other people, and altogether get things wrong. God, in contrast, is unable to make human errors. He is perfect, which makes Him so completely different from us that He's worthy of our worship.

It's His holiness and His perfection that requires holiness and perfection from us before we can enter into His presence. He can't allow sin into His heaven. There is no sin in heaven. However, our perfect, holy Father made a way for imperfect humans to join Him after this life on earth is over. He provided His perfect, holy Son, Jesus to take our place. He covered us in His righteousness, His perfection, so that we can enter into God's presence. This is the great news about God's holiness. He doesn't just demand perfection, He provides it for us to receive as a gift.

It's His holiness that also makes Him good. It's His goodness that also makes Him loving. It's His love that saved us.

Holy Father, I could never thank you enough for your free gift of salvation in Jesus. You made a way for this imperfect, sinful person to become righteous through Christ and in Him I can enter heaven. Thank you. Thank you. Thank you. You are holy. You are righteous. You are good.

Amen

He is just

2 Thessalonians 1:6 (NIV 1984) God is just: He will pay back trouble to those who trouble you

Do you have any enemies? Has anyone ever done anything to you that made you want revenge? Did you make it happen? Why is it that we would do something like that to those who have wronged us? Perhaps it's a little bit of the image of God in us. He loves justice.

It's human nature to want people to pay for the wrongs they've done. Well, unless those people are ourselves...then we have a slightly more lenient view toward justice. But it's not up to us to make sure that people get what's coming to them. One reason for that is because we're often not really after justice, just revenge. We just want to feel better about the situation by seeing the wrongdoer suffer.

But God isn't about revenge. He isn't about payback. He's a holy and righteous Judge who knows what true justice is all about. He knows how to give the proper sentence for the sin. Lest we forget, we're all worthy of His judgment and His punishment.

It's His just nature that makes a sacrifice for atonement necessary. It's because He is a truly righteous Judge that we deserve death and eternal suffering in hell. But it's His loving nature that made sure we could be judged on the merits of another. If God can only accept perfection into His presence and judges based on our deeds, then without Christ we're doomed. But because Jesus took our sentence and served our time, we are free. The just God of heaven gave us a break, not because He isn't fair, but because He is love.

Thank you, Father, for being fair and just. I'm so glad that I can trust you to judge rightly and sentence exactly as deserved.

Amen

He Judges

Isaiah 33:22 For the Lord is our judge; the Lord is our lawgiver; the Lord is our king; he will save us.

The bad news is, God is our judge. The good news is, the Judge is on our side. If we're in Christ, we have a mediator who acts on our behalf to keep the Judge's wrath from us. The Judge sees His Son in us and rules in our favor.

Which of us is worthy of judging another? We've all committed sins and are guilty of our own transgressions. How could we judge anyone with so many strikes against us? But God isn't like us. The Judge is without sin, without blemish. He is holy, and only one who is holy is worthy to judge. He alone holds the right to hand down a verdict.

One day we'll all stand before Him and He'll make His ruling. We're either not-guilty because we've believed on Christ for our salvation, or we're guilty because we tried to be good enough on our own and didn't measure up. Where will you stand on the final judgement day? Will you be acquitted of all charges because Christ your mediator stands between you and the Judge, or will you find yourself accused without counsel to defend you?

Thank you, Father, for finding me "not guilty" in Christ Jesus. Thank you for sending Him to be judged in my place so that I might be free.

Amen

He is awesome

Nahum 1:5 The mountains quake before him; the hills melt; the earth heaves before him, the world and all who dwell in it.

How big is God? How great is God? How wonderful is God? If you had a million years to answer these questions, it wouldn't be enough time. There wouldn't be enough words.

The late song-writer and singer, Rich Mullins, made it popular to say that "our God is an awesome God," but mixed in with the overuse of this word as slang in previous generations, we've lost what it actually means to be "awesome."

When we think of God existing before time and yet knowing our names prior to the creation of anything, it's amazing. When we think of how really powerful God is to not only answer our prayers but to provide us things that we didn't even know we needed, it's astounding. When we sit and ponder just how big He is, and how small we are, it's nothing short of awesome.

These things, they strike in us a sense of wonder, a dumbfounded state that is indescribable. We stand in awe of our Creator, who would make all of the things we see and all of the things we can't see, and think about how He loves little ol' us. This is beyond our ability to even really understand. That's why it inspires awe. That's why it's awesome.

Our God IS an awesome God.

Father, I stand amazed by you. There's no way I could ever comprehend, in this lifetime, all that you are. You simply are awesome.

Amen

He is patient

1 Peter 3:9 The Lord is not slow to fulfill his promise as some count slowness, but is patient toward you, not wishing that any should perish, but that all should reach repentance.

Have you ever messed up? Have you ever committed the same sin over and over, seemingly unable to get ahold of things? How about being disobedient to God in something you know He's told you to do? Maybe in those moments you thought God must be pretty upset with you over your repeated actions. Maybe you thought He must be ready to give up on you.

The thing is, God doesn't live in our time. He's working on things, whether we see what's going on or not. He's not sitting up in heaven, waiting for us to make a move before He can proceed. He's not becoming impatient when we struggle with sin or with obedience. He's working on each of us, in His own time, and He'll bring all things to completion‡.

God has a plan and He knows what needs to happen in order for it to work out.   While we do need to be obedient and follow His commands, He will do what needs to be done with or without us. He's patient in waiting for us to do what He wills, but because it works in us to bring us closer to Him, not because He needs our help.

He's patient in bringing all things to an end because there are still those who have yet to respond to His invitation to receive eternal life in Jesus. He's patient because He's loving.

---

‡ Philippians 1:6

Father, thank you for taking your time with me. I know that I am often impatient, but your timing is perfect and you know exactly when to take action. Thank you for allowing me grace in the times that I've been less than patient in waiting.

Amen

He Loves

John 3:16 For God so loved the world, that he gave his only Son,
that whoever believes in him should not perish but have eternal life.

God isn't just another person in life who goes around saying things
He doesn't mean. God cannot lie and He does not make promises He
doesn't keep. When He says He loves us, He doesn't just leave it at
that. He demonstrates it.

Do we understand what it means that God loves us? Do we grasp the
heaviness of the fact that the one who created all things has affection
for us? That He thinks about us? That He has a plan for us? He
works in our lives, shaping us to be who He created us to be. He
disciplines us when we've done wrong, just as a father disciplines his
children so that they'll learn right from wrong. God shows His love
by being involved in our lives.

In an act that could never be confused for anything but love, God sent
His Son to die a painful death of suffering on a cross, taking on our
sin and giving us His righteousness, so that He could have a
relationship with us. This act was not because we had done anything
to earn His love, but because He just loved us that much.

When we struggle in life, when things just don't seem to make sense,
when we feel like no one loves us, we can look at all that God has
done for us. Look to the forgiveness you've received in Christ, to the
wonderful promises God has made, and to the Holy Spirit He's placed
in your life to comfort and guide you. He loves you so much that He
can't stay away from you. He's crazy about you.

Thank you, Father, for your love. Your love never ends, never depends on me to earn it, never ceases to amaze. Keep me mindful of your love for me, Father, and help me to show others your love.

Amen

ABOUT THE AUTHOR

Matthew J. Cochran is a devoted father of three and a former Marine (1998-2003) who finds his calling in leading people into a deeper relationship with God through Jesus Christ. His approach to this is two-fold: shine light on the supremacy of Christ through the Gospel and lead others to trust God in all things.

Matt has served in children's ministry, new believers' ministry, and young adults ministry over the years. His experience leading Marines, helping to plant new churches and with discipling young people has allowed the Spirit to open Matt's eyes to the need for servant leadership and helping others to serve Christ with compassion. He's passionate about being a dad, eating great food, and spending time with the love of his life, Sarah.

FOLLOW MJC ONLINE

Twitter: @matthewjcochran

Facebook: @matthewjcochran

iTunes: MJC Podcast & Fragile Freedom

Blog: www.matthewjcochran.com

Amazon: www.amazon.com/author/matthewjcochran

NOTES

NOTES

NOTES

www.ingramcontent.com/pod-product-compliance
Lightning Source LLC
Chambersburg PA
CBHW071927020426
42331CB00010B/2759